The Positive YOu!

Anita Papas

turning**point**
B O O K S

Published by Turning Point Books
15th Floor, Concorde Building
Dunan Street, Verdun
Beirut, Lebanon
P.O. Box: 14-6613
Tel: 00961 1 752 100
www.tpbooksonline.com

First edition: April, 2009
First edition, second printing: August, 2009
First edition, third reprint: June, 2011
First edition, fourth reprint: November, 2013

Layout and graphic design: Rima Rifai

ISBN 978-9953-0-1396-1

Printing: **edots**

To Alexis,
Thank you for believing in me. Your love, loyalty, friendship, unconditional support and constant encouragement have made me who I am today.
I respect you, admire you and treasure the time we share together. You have made every day special, every journey worthwhile and I look forward to spending the rest of our lives together.

To Eddie,
You make me proud in every possible way a parent can be! Your intelligence, creativity, honesty, passion, sense of humor, love of life, just to mention a few, make up the wonderful boy that you are! Bringing you up has been the most exciting experience in my life.

To Christina,
You are the sunshine in my life. You radiate love, beauty and peace everywhere you go. You fill my heart with joy, my eyes with admiration, my ears with the sound of your sweet words. You have simply turned my world into a living dream. I am forever thankful to have you as my daughter.

Contents

Biography

Anita Papas is a clinical psychologist whose hunger for knowledge was evident at an early age. She continually sought answers about God, human existence and the meaning of life, and was unable to satisfy her natural curiosity more often than not. "We were intrigued by her inquisitive mind," her mother remembers. At university, Anita spent most of her time in the college library reading whatever she could get her hands on. She was devoted to psychology and was an honors student throughout her college years. Her dream to become a clinical psychologist had to be put on hold temporarily when, in 1994, she met and married her prince charming, Alexis Papas, a successful businessman with whom she has two wonderful children, Eddie and Christina. It seemed that life could not get much better for Anita - except for her yet unrealized dream. In 2002, she decided to go back to college to study for her Master's degree. She graduated in 2005 from Haigazian University and has been practicing psychology ever since.

Her passion for writing was a gift she discovered early on. As a teenager, her emotions, internal turmoil as well as rebellions were expressed in lines of poetry. At university, she most enjoyed presenting her case studies, during which she did not leave any detail to the imagination. She told a friend that along with the degree in clinical psychology, she deserved one for creative writing!

The Positive You! is Anita's first book and she is in the process of writing a complementary sequel, *The Positive Us!*, which deals with relationship issues with friends, your significant other and families.

Preface

Have you ever had an open, honest and meaningful conversation with a total stranger sitting next to you on an airplane or a bus? Knowing that you will never again come across this person, did you somehow feel free to reveal certain thoughts and ideas that you may hold back from sharing with the people closest to you? Did you think that this person, having no past or preconceived ideas about you, would be less biased and more objective towards your arguments than your loved ones? Just before starting to write this book a similar incident happened to me.

I was trapped for almost three hours with a group of 50 other people waiting for a plane, which gave me the opportunity to have an interesting conversation with a total stranger. We had a lot of time to talk and exchange ideas and I mentioned that I was interested in writing a book. I related to her the major ideas and thoughts that would make up my book and she sat there listening to me attentively, interested in all I had to say. At the end of our conversation, she told me, "You would be very selfish if you did not share all this with others."

Since that day, this statement helped me overcome all the obstacles and difficulties in bringing this book to life. Ironically, the writing of *The Positive You!* coincided with some of the saddest and most tearful moments in my life. It was like a force majeure-unexpected turn of events came up, family health issues surfaced and accidents took place. Just thinking about these incidents as I write this sends shivers down my spine. I was forced to interrupt my work for weeks, sometimes even months. Despite all the negativity surrounding me, I tried to keep my spirits high - the idea of quitting never crossed my mind, as I had a message to deliver. I kept going and, hopefully, put together a book that will make a difference in the reader's life. I am quite certain that most of us are already aware of what I have written, but to know something and to integrate it in one's daily life are two different things. It is important to remember that our problems are surmountable and that with a little bit of effort we can overcome just about anything. The thought, the one thought, that I will never let go of is: "Everything will be okay."

Introduction

There are basically two breeds of people: the optimists and the pessimists. They live in two very different worlds, where exactly the same events take place every day at the same time. The life of the former is full of joy, gratitude and hope, whereas the life of the latter is full of malcontent, resentment and chaos. These two breeds from two different worlds seem very much alike, so much so that it is difficult to tell them apart - except when they talk. It is then that the difference is immediately detected.

This is the story of each and every one of us, our families and immediate circles. It is the story of every living soul who was once part of this life: the humble, the greedy, the hero, the villain, the victim and the survivor. It is the story of all those who built our world today and of life and how we embrace it as well as the titles we give to our own existence and the marks we wish to leave behind for immortality.

The pain of observing human beings tormenting themselves with ideas that are nothing but the fruit of their own minds was always distasteful for me. In my own family, my father was an ardent optimist, as opposed to my mother, who was the constant worrier. At an early age, I noticed that even though my mother and father lived in the same house, raised the same children, survived the same wars, entertained in the same social circles, each had a very different story to tell.

As a clinical psychologist, I have been witnessing that individuals are victims of their own thoughts, ideas and ideals. My role is allowing them to see that having a different attitude, or simply giving different explanations to the same experiences, will change the whole perspective of an event.

Ever since, people have always strived for the ultimate goal: happiness. We all want acceptance, wealth, careers, recognition and physical beauty in order to achieve happiness. Happiness itself is an aim, not a means through which we wish to obtain something else. Yet, we wonder why people are less happy, less satisfied even when they have obtained all the above characteristics or positions. Why on earth are some people simply cheerful while others are constantly moody? Why is it that some of us concentrate on the good in people and situations while others only choose to witness the bad?

It is no secret that some of us are just not natural optimists. We somehow fail to see the glass half full and dwell on the negatives. We fear and worry about losing what we have achieved, thus, we get into vicious cycles of negativity, especially in the face of adversity, when it often becomes harder to maintain one's usual composure. What are we supposed to do in such circumstances?

The good news is that optimism can be learned! We can teach and train ourselves to be positive. Positivism can even be contagious. Just as dwelling on negative events can lead to depression, dwelling on things that have gone well can really boost your mood.

Today, I have decided to put my every thought into writing, my every experience into practice, and do all I can to help unite the two separate worlds to form one that is more positive, happy and optimistic.

CHAPTER ONE

Love yourself

*"*Each morning when I awake, I experience again a supreme pleasure – that of being Salvador Dali *"*

Salvador Dali 1904-1989

Love yourself, be in love with your own self, adore every inch of the marvelous you. Pamper yourself. Be proud of how you look. Be grateful for your body and all the great functions it performs.

To become a positive you, it is of utmost importance that you love yourself. Love starts from within. When we love ourselves, we are able to love others. It is only through discovering our own feelings that we can reach out to others. We sometimes try to find outside ourselves the meaning of life and the value of love, or simply have the need for external sources to remind us or drive us towards our goals. We search for answers from others regarding issues concerning ourselves. I believe all the answers lie inside us - all creativity, imagination, motivation, energy, it is all in us. However tempting or promising outer sources may seem, everything you need and you will ever need is all in you! Have you realized that we constantly seek validation and confirmation for our own convictions? Even when we seek advice from others, deep inside we wish the advice given to us is the one we are secretly already wishing for in our hearts. When you discover yourself fully and love yourself, you will be the driving force in your life. You will be and you will have all the answers. All the power you need is in you. Nobody, yes nobody, is capable of loving you more than you!

Learning to love yourself

" Self-love is not so vile a sin as self-neglecting "

William Shakespeare 1564-1616

Most of us were raised to please others - whether our parents, teachers, friends or other family members. But, as an adult, there is a limit to how much energy we can spend on pleasing others before it affects our desires or depletes our resources.

The Positive Y⌣u!

For most of us, genuine self-love seems so elusive - not so easy to achieve or even to grasp. Putting our loved ones' happiness above our own is so common. We are only too ready to sacrifice our needs to accommodate theirs and so reluctant to place our wishes above theirs. But, I have something else to tell you: you come first, so put yourself first!

Back at university, there was a certain Mrs. X in one of our case studies. Mrs. X was 50 years old, and throughout her life she was the perfect daughter, the perfect employee, the perfect wife, the perfect mother and, as she sat in the psychologist's clinic, she was also the perfect patient. Somewhere along the way, Mrs. X forgot to be perfect to herself, to her own needs, desires, wishes and caprices. She denied herself what she was more than willing to give others. It is sad but true that such people are taken for granted - but, who is really to blame? If she herself did not take the time to realize she was not being fair to her own self, should we expect others to do so? Each one of the parties involved only saw one aspect of Mrs. X: daughter, employee, wife, mother, etc. So, who is more responsible for recognizing her needs than Mrs. X herself? I hate to blame the victim, but after reading this anecdotal case, I am certain you will agree with me.

Imagine, just for a moment, putting yourself first. It may sound selfish, but it isn't really. It's not about abandoning everyone else, it's simply about honoring your own wellbeing. After all, how can you truly give all that you are capable of giving if you are not properly taken care of, rested or happy?

Loving yourself is about treating yourself as you would someone precious to you. Remember, love is not merely a feeling, it is a choice. So, make the choice to love yourself. After all, who deserves it more? This is not selfishness. This is an act of self-love.

Loving yourself means actively taking care of every aspect of your person. It is evident in things as trivial as nourishing and taking care of your body, breaking up an abusive, unfulfilling relationship, and reaching your maximum potential.

The relationship you have with yourself is the central relationship in your life. At the core of all the components that make up your life - such as family, friends, work and community - stands you. That is why your relationship with yourself is crucial for the creation, continuity and success of all the other relationships and elements in your life.

Accept yourself as you are right now

> " To love oneself is the beginning of a life-long romance "
>
> *Oscar Wilde 1854-1900*

Loving yourself means accepting yourself and being happy with who you are. It is like an agreement with yourself to appreciate, validate, accept and support who you are at this very moment. This is the key: you should accept even those parts of yourself that you want to change. Until you accept yourself as the person you are, you cannot truly be content.

A common, or rather paradoxical, belief among people is that if they actually accept themselves as they are, they will not work on becoming more of who they want to be. The counter argument is very simple: acceptance is the first step in the process of change. Why? Because it gives us something solid to stand on as we reach for more.

We hate ourselves for being fat to get ourselves to diet. We judge ourselves unfavorably with the hope that it will motivate us to change. We sometimes even punish ourselves for not keeping our promises. In short, we hope that if we feel bad enough about ourselves, then we will push ourselves to change.

The Positive You!

Self-condemnation, self-degradation and put-downs are all too common, but lead nowhere. We all have off days - you're not alone when facing challenging times. Unfortunately, all this consumes our energy, which might have otherwise been used to make changes.

We all want more from ourselves - we want to improve, whether physically, mentally, academically, professionally or socially. But remember, the area that you find unsatisfactory and would like to ameliorate does not constitute your core self and does not deem your entire being unsatisfactory. Learn to separate.

Take a walk on the path of learning to accept yourself just as you are. Despite perfectionism, shame, body image, fears and worries, have the courage to explore and accept yourself. On the flip side of your deepest fears are your greatest strengths and gifts. Accept and love yourself unconditionally - that is the true philosophy of happiness.

Treat yourself kindly

> " You, yourself, as much as anybody in the entire universe, deserve your love and affection "
>
> *Buddha 563-483 BC*

We all seek the company of people who are kind and considerate towards us. We expect our friends to be understanding and accepting of us, our partners to be loving and forgiving, our family to be open and honest. But how many of these virtues do we actually extend to ourselves? How kind are we to ourselves? Why is it that we constantly deny ourselves the very things we expect from others? Why do we hope others will respect our needs when we don't? Once again, it starts from within. You ought to grant yourself all good deeds and acts before expecting others to do it for you. No one is more capable of loving you and giving you exactly what you need more than you are!

The ways you can be nice to yourself are infinite, starting with simple gestures, like treating yourself with occasional gifts, a special dinner, or a long overdue vacation. You can also reward yourself after a hard day's work, a difficult exam or a challenging project. Try celebrating important events and prioritizing - and I do mean prioritizing - what really matters in your life. Cultivate meaningful, respectful relationships, be it with immediate family, extended family, friends, or neighbors. There are countless ways to make it count. Depending on your own likes and needs, once again you know best.

I had a friend whose list of Christmas gifts started off with her own name! Every single Christmas, she bought something really special for herself. She even went through the trouble of having it wrapped and put under the Christmas tree and would only open it on Christmas Eve. This may not mean much to you, but I am sure you can find your own special way of occasionally treating yourself nicely.

Treating yourself kindly includes self-talk. However, be careful to speak to yourself in ways that are more kind and less harsh or judgmental. Stop the critic inside you, the internal voice within each of us that likes to remind us of our limitations or fear of failure. When faced with a challenge, make the conscious decision to trust in your abilities and to give yourself positive affirmations, such as "yes I can do it" and "I will make it"! Negative self-talk only sabotages our best efforts and wastes our full potential.

Remember your personal breakthroughs and not just your failures. We all have proud moments of high achievement. Do not treat them as if they happened in somebody else's life - it is one thing being modest, but another being downright passive about personal victories. This particular point is evident when visiting people's homes. For example, when visiting a neighbor, you may see a framed picture nailed to the living room wall showing him very proudly holding a huge tuna along with his fishing partners on a boat, smiling at the camera. In another house, another living room, you may come across the pictures of the happy couple who managed to travel and visit all seven wonders of the modern world. Other homes will tell you other stories - the proud parents with their graduating son, the daughter on the day of her prom, a long line of frames of grandchildren. Yes, these are our achievements in life; let us not forget them or take them for granted. Remember them; make them visible to remind you to be appreciative and thankful every single day.

While we all have our moments of self-doubt and hesitation, why wait around for someone else to give you an uplifting and empowering personal compliment when nobody knows you better than you do? When your personal power starts to run low, be the first one to give it a boost. Rediscover your overlooked personal strengths and learn to laugh at your own flaws too.

My sister and I live in the same neighborhood, but somehow, with our busy lifestyles, we don't get to see much of each other. But, what is sacred for both of us is our daily phone conversations. It is the biggest relief of the day - they are purely therapeutic. I call it "catharsis" for the simple reason that my sister and I somehow learned to laugh at just about anything. No matter what has occurred during the day, good or bad, and no matter how angry I am, just talking about it with my sister, with no exceptions, always makes me laugh, turning even the worst of events into one of our own personal jokes. With my sister, this is so natural. Situations seem lighter, less serious, funnier and even memorable. I know whatever happens, I can laugh it out with her, and I can assure you, it is a great feeling. Of course, we get our usual complaints from children from both households - my nephews tell me when their mother is laughing out loud, they know it is me on the other end of the line!

The lesson here is not to take yourself too seriously. Learn to laugh at your mistakes and bad situations, as this will prevent us from being too harsh on ourselves when facing disappointment, or when we don't measure up to our own high expectations.

It is of paramount importance to note that one of the people who will not and should not let you down is yourself. So, go ahead, compliment yourself when you are down, remind yourself of your every successful venture, pamper yourself, laugh at your own flaws, set your own rules and principles, build your own character, have faith in your abilities, believe in yourself and, most of all, love yourself, and trust me, the rest will follow.

Love your life: the miracle of life

> " There are only two ways to live your life. One is as though nothing is a miracle. The other as though everything is a miracle "

Albert Einstein 1879-1955

Life is a miracle, live it. Life is beautiful, be grateful for it. Every sunrise you witness is a miracle; every breath you take in your perfectly harmonious body is a miracle; every single mother giving birth to a child is a miracle; every word we utter is a miracle - we should never cease to believe that.

Think of the miracle of being able to taste and enjoy something delicious. Think of the soft kiss of a child on your cheek. Think of the inner contentment as you listen to beautiful music. Think of the mesmerized feeling you experience when close to a loved one. Aren't all these miracles of life? Why do we take them for granted? Why is it that with the realization of a loss we come to appreciate it more? Why can't we be more aware and conscious of all the things we already have rather than what we would like to have? To begin with, let us all be grateful for our lives.

The more you appreciate the life given you - the greatest gift - the more you love yourself and life. You have to make the choice: you can grumble about your health, or you can rejoice that you are alive. You can mourn your lack of friends, or you can excitedly set out to discover new relationships. You can whine because you have to go to work, or you can shout for joy because you have a job. You can lament over past mistakes, or you can judge them to be a learning experience. You can complain about the banalities of everyday life, or you can be thankful to have a life. Life stretches ahead of us, waiting to be shaped and we are the sculptors that do the shaping. It is up to us to choose what kind of life we want to live.

The miracle starts from within, with the belief that we are individuals worthy of love, life and happiness. Each and every one of us is a miracle because we are each unique. There are over six billion people living on this planet and you cannot spot two exactly the same. Isn't that a miracle?

Love your life. Your life is yours. Don't live your life like an explanation, live it like an exclamation! Celebrate life, celebrate yourself. You are a unique individual, given the gift of life. Your life is like the virgin snow lying in front of you and it is up to you to leave your own special mark as you go along.

Count your blessings

" Men are slower to recognize blessings than evils "

Titus Livius 59 BC-AD 17

Sometimes, we fall in the easy trap of focusing on what's wrong so that we fail to see all the things that are right. Take the time to stop and think how much you have going for you. Be grateful for everything you have in your life. Recognize how lucky you are. Rather than focusing on what you do not have, focus on what you do have.

We all adapt to certain lifestyles - no matter how lavish or comfortable, sooner or later we become accustomed to it and treat it as if it is normal, everyone has it or that it is no big deal. Something as simple as owning a car should be appreciated when you start considering the alternatives, so do not take things for granted.

Not everyone has a listening ear when they need to vent out their anger, so be appreciative if you do. Not all of us were bestowed with all five senses, so be grateful if you are. Not all are lucky enough to have a mother and father while growing up, so no matter what your issues are with your parents, be glad you had them. The number of things you can be grateful for in life are countless.

Learning to be grateful and saying thank you are so essential in our recognition and acceptance of our current lives, no matter what the circumstances. Life is worth it despite the severe trials. Be thankful and glad for what you are and then try and build on it, ameliorate it.

It is said that for every proverb, there is one that claims the exact opposite. Using this idea, I would advise to look at the big picture in life and count your blessings. Let every-day banalities be just what they are: everyday banalities. Look at where you are headed - even if you don't get every single endeavor right, detach yourself from everyday mundane matters, because the big picture is what you ought to be focusing on. The opposite is also true. Everyday details are also part of your life - enjoy the noisy confusion and everyday trivialities and make the most out of them.

Don't be so taken with where life is taking you; navigate through life, enjoy the process, make the most out of your journey, even if you are uncertain about where you are headed. So, no matter what you choose to concentrate on, whether the big picture or everyday details, don't forget to be happy and positive, and don't forget to live! Don't postpone your happiness. Be grateful for what you are now, today, and enjoy it to the fullest. The only true way you will be able to achieve this is to be appreciative of all that life has granted you already.

CHAPTER TWO

Be the best of you

"" We know what we are, but know not what we may be ""

William Shakespeare 1564-1616

The only person you really need to compete with is yourself. Try to be the best version of yourself and reach your highest potential. Do not make unnecessary comparisons to people around you. No matter how intelligent, beautiful, successful or famous you are, there is someone out there who has more than you. If you live a life of constantly comparing yourself to others you will never be happy with what you have. However, when we are always improving ourselves, the only measure being our own potential, we will feel rewarded, fulfilled and may end up reaching undreamed of heights.

Easier said than done, I agree, especially if early in life some of us often received negative comments such as, "Why can't you be more like your brother?" or experienced a cruel school system, where students are only numbers to be evaluated, compared and ranked. Each child feels as big and important as their grades allow. Schools are breeding grounds for comparisons and we register all these messages because, after all, these are our very first experiences in the social world. We consider them correct, follow them and execute them, until one day we are totally consumed by them.

We reach our teenage years with the need to conform, afraid of disapproval. Our peers are what we want to be. We want to fit in, unwilling to show ourselves as different because we assume it is safer to be one of them. Teenagers have a vague sense of identity. That is why fashion, trends and the latest crazes are so easily adopted by them. As we approach adulthood, our sense of self and individuality becomes clearer to us. Unique traits of personality emerge, distinct characteristics surface. In other words, grownups are much more aware of their identity and sense of self.

Unfortunately, some of us "adults" fall into the never ending road of comparisons. This is where, without even noticing, an internal battle takes place, in which no matter how many victories you achieve, you still feel you are losing the war.

The Positive Y∪u!

The only competition you have is you

" Envy is an insult to oneself "

Yevgeny Yevtushenko 1933-

We are introduced to the concept of competition early on in life and develop an unhealthy view of it - namely, that competition only involves those outside us, be it a sibling, fellow student or friend. Today, I challenge that idea and say that your competition is with yourself and no one else.

I always believed that I had to be the best at everything I did - when I worked out at the gym, I had to be the fittest, if I walked in to a party, I had to be the center of attention, and I would not feel comfortable or enjoy myself until I mentally checked out and successfully eliminated any possible competition. If I was playing a game, I had to win, and anytime I felt I could not compete, I would simply retreat, as I could not face being second-best. Sound familiar?

My personal crusade went on until my post-graduate studies, when I was faced with a very special student. She was very bright and scored the highest grades with little effort. It was one of those situations that I could not retreat from - I was literally stuck. I hated every session, every exam; I worked so hard and still she performed better than I did. I tried to convince myself that this was the only thing she was better at, grades, that I was more charming and more popular than she was, but still, I had this horrible pain in my stomach. This feeling lasted until one day, I went to her and told her how highly I thought of her. I admited how much I admired her for her intelligence and all the good work she was doing. Then came the unexpected - she started pointing out all the good things she saw in me and how much she envied how organized I was and how well I prepared my presentations.

Then, and only then, did I realize I was only harming myself, and the reality of the situation hit me: all those negative feelings and comparisons led to nothing but frustration, bad feelings, resentment and uneasiness. In a nutshell, all it amounted to was wasted energy. I am forever grateful to her for making me realize this with her openness and honesty.

Today, if I could turn back the clock, I would handle the whole situation differently. Rather than comparing myself to others, I would turn inwards and find the best in me to work on, to ameliorate and to perfect. Don't worry about what you haven't got in the way of talent. Find out what you do have. Everything we need is in us, so there is no need to look outside ourselves. Just work and focus on your strong points, make them better until you reach your potential. Nobody is perfect at everything; we all have our own special side and it is up to us to discover it and maximize it. Don't dwell on the negatives, it won't get you anywhere. Be optimistic and expect the best from your own efforts, and you will surely reap the benefits.

Jealousy and envy: turning them to your advantage

> " To cure jealousy is to see it for what it is, a dissatisfaction with self "
>
> *Joan Didion 1934-*

Jealousy is innate and demonstrates itself in many ways early on in life. It is part of the human condition and, at times, even a means of survival. Perhaps the most flagrant of examples of pure jealousy came from my seven year old daughter - when I asked her if she wanted a little brother or sister, she immediately felt her position being threatened. Having an older brother, she wanted to guarantee her place as the youngest in the family. It was as though her whole world fell apart and she looked at me with tearful big blue eyes and answered, "No!!! I will be too jealous! I only want me!"

Although sometimes used synonymously, envy and jealousy have different meanings and it is important to clarify the difference. Feelings of jealousy always appear to stem from one's fear that they will lose something that they already have, most often love relationships. Envy, on the other hand, is to view the well-being of others with distress. According to Aristotle, envy is pain at the good fortune of others. To be envious is to cross the line into malice. The object of one's envy can be a material possession, a quality or virtue, an achievement or success, a relationship or any number of things.

I call energy wasted on envy negative energy because it creates an unnecessary mental and emotional turmoil defeating our own sense of being. However, when all our energy is directed towards our own interests and goals and used constructively, we become more efficient and, thus, more successful in all our endeavors.

Why are some people better equipped to turn these negative emotions into a motivating force while others find that they get so eaten by it?

Turning unhealthy feelings of jealousy or envy into healthy feelings is accomplished by identifying and challenging irrational beliefs, by showing yourself that they are false, illogical and self-defeating. By reframing and de-demonizing these difficult emotions and revealing their potentially creative power, we empower ourselves. Thinking about what your jealousy tells you about yourself can help you learn more about yourself, what you fear and how you may be fooling yourself. Think about what is reflected when you feel jealous of someone else. Is it a fear of rejection? Or, not being good enough? Ask yourself what is this jealousy revealing to me? How can I grow from this insight?

Your individuality is something to take pride in. Rediscover YOU. We are all blessed with some special talent, ability, virtue - we all excel in certain things in which others don't. It is time to define your own reality and create the life that will make you happy. Rather than blindly following society's definition of success, create your own standard to measure your achievements. We can't all squeeze ourselves into the same mold and we should not want to. Therefore, it is of great importance to be able to develop your special gift and work on it. Focus on being better, even just a little bit more each day, and soon enough you will master it.

Focusing on the best you

 " We are all something, but none of us are everything "

Blaise Pascal 1623-1662

Each of us has been blessed with unique qualities. No one else has lived through precisely the same circumstances, possesses exactly the same qualities, or thinks the same thoughts. We love, appreciate and prioritize vastly different things. Because of this, it is nearly impossible to fairly compare one person to another, and yet so many people stake their happiness on how they fare when measured against a sibling, neighbor, colleague or even a celebrity. We sometimes even tend to compare the worst trait in us with the best of someone else - like, for example, comparing your ugly voice with the vocals of a celebrated opera singer, or your sagging tummy with the muscular body of an Olympic athlete. You may find these examples ridiculous, nevertheless, we are prone to making such unjust comparisons.

If you keep focusing on everyone else's journey, you're going to stop paying attention to your own. We need to live our own lives, following our own unique plan and purpose. This requires us to be passionate and proactive, taking charge of our thoughts, lives, and the direction we are taking. Think about who you are and what you are becoming. As George Bernard Shaw put it, "Life isn't about finding yourself. Life is about creating yourself." Create the best you. I can't emphasize this enough - you are the captain of your own ship. You have to be solid internally, or else you will be pushed away with every flow or current.

The Positive You!

It is because we are different that each of us is special. Greatness lies in following your own path. Strive for uniqueness, not conformity. Find your own particular talent. The paradox is that often having less is having more. For when we have less wealth and talent, or are blessed with less beauty, we often have more drive, ambition, direction, purpose and adventure.

It also needs to be said that envy is ignorance of the problems others have. The subject of your envy may have an internal turmoil - like being insecure or worried about the future - or have relationship and other problems. It is only your ignorance and lack of knowledge regarding their internal conflicts that makes you envy them.

Focus on the best you and stop wasting time comparing yourself to others. You, and only you, are capable of revealing the best of you to the world. If you deny that to yourself, who do you expect will do that for you? It all starts with believing in yourself and celebrating your unique, individual and special characteristics.

Be above it all

"For self is a sea boundless and measureless"

Gibran Khalil Gibran 1883-1931

It was my sophomore year at college and, as usual, preparations were being made for the election of 'Miss University'. As each one was cheering the other to participate, for a moment, I was tempted to join the contest. Later that day, before heading back home, I went to my locker, only to find an anonymous note that read: "Anita, don't go for it. Don't stand up there and be compared to any other girl! You know exactly who you are."

At first, I thought it was someone who was threatened by my participation. Later on, when I really gave it thought,

I realized it was concern that led this person to write the note. I was moved. I took this anonymous advice back then and have been carrying it with me ever since. It made me realize that I did not need a group of people to judge my physical beauty or intellectual ability. I did not need their approval to feel I was indeed the best that I could be, irrespective of what others thought of me. I have no limits, no boundaries for who I am and what I can achieve.

Do not let others specify what you are good at and, more importantly, what you are not good at. It is not up to others to decide your potential. Sometimes, a negative remark, a false assessment or judgment made by others can hold us back for years. Erase all, if any, negative messages you received about yourself. No one has the right to judge or belittle you. Remember, you know yourself best; in your heart you know who you are, so don't let anyone take that power from you. Surround yourself with people who boost, encourage and have faith in you. After all, you cannot be in an environment in which the current is against you. For a short while, you will resist, but eventually, you will crumble and fall. Live in a sound, healthy and nurturing atmosphere. Surround yourself with positive people.

It is okay not to be perfect

66 Have no fear of perfection – you'll never reach it 99

Salvador Dali 1904-1989

A few years ago, we were preparing for our usual annual summer family vacation. As usual, we were trying to be well-equipped so as not to leave behind the necessities, like medication, clothes, the favorite toys and biscuits, etc. At the end, it felt like we were moving the whole house with us, because everything seemed necessary.

As our camcorder was replaced by a newer, technologically advanced model, my husband gave the old one to our then nine year old son. It was only after leaving the house to the airport that I noticed my son had brought his newly acquired camcorder. Every once in a while throughout the trip, I noticed he was preoccupied with the camera, but I did not give it much importance.

After we got back from our trip, we went over all the photos, and of course watched the home videos of the vacation. It was simply perfect - broad smiles on our faces, peaceful day trips that all went according to plan, wonderful dinners, when children were spotlessly clean and we were all dressed in matching colors and smiles. It was simply beautiful. I still had a broad contented smile on my face when my husband told me, "Look how creative our little one has been!"

My son, Eddie, with his own camcorder, without our knowledge, had filmed us at the most unexpected times. He captured moments, such as when our luggage was late and we had to claim it. My husband's anger was mounting by the minute because of the language barrier. He also filmed my four year old daughter yelling, terrified of a big clown by a restaurant, and even the first day at the hotel, when we were all searching for one item or the other in four suitcases, which had become our only link to home. In other words, he filmed us in the worst of situations. We had a completely different version of the trip played back to us - it was far from perfect, but it was still wonderful. This was our trip in its entirety, not just the clean clothes and smiles. We cherish that film and have enjoyed watching it over and over, more than any other home movie taken by me or my husband. My son taught me that things need not be perfect for us to enjoy them and could not have chosen a better way to persuade me.

Life is not perfect and if you try and pretend that you will attain perfection, you will be in for the biggest disappointment of your life. Learn to enjoy your life with its imperfections - trust me, you will make your life and the life of those around you much easier.

CHAPTER THREE

Your mind, your world

"Our life is what our thoughts make it"

Marcus Aurelius 121-180

The Positive You!

Have you ever stopped and thought that your mind has no limits? That in your mind you can be any place you desire at any time? That no one has any control over what you think other than you?

The freest you will ever be is in your mind. Our mind is ours alone and it is the most private part of our being. Why then, would we want to pollute it with unnecessary worries? Why would we want to burden it with distortions? Why would we spend even one minute with some negative thought?

Every perception, word or action is the product of our own mind. Every intention, deed and effort is the direct outcome of our thoughts. Even feelings emerge from our thoughts.

How your thoughts create your feelings

> " Except our own thoughts, there is nothing absolutely in our power "
>
> *Rene Descartes 1596-1650*

The session I really love and enjoy in therapy is the one in which I explain to my clients the essential techniques of cognitive therapy. Cognitive therapy is a structured, short-term, present-oriented form of psychotherapy. The basic assumption of cognitive therapy is that by modifying dysfunctional thoughts, negative attitudes and irrational beliefs, we modify moods and, thus, behavior. It may look very simple to most people, however, the astonished look on the faces of my clients made me realize that something as simple as a thought preceeding feelings had never even occurred to some.

The therapist seeks in a variety of techniques to produce cognitive restructuring - change in the client's thinking, interpretation and beliefs - in order to bring about enduring emotional and behavioral change. By educating the client about the cognitive model, he or she feels more in control of his or her emotions.

Feelings are internal experiences of emotion. For example, I may feel happy, sad, anxious or confused, but what I should realize is that any one of these feelings is the direct result of what I was thinking - in other words, my cognitions. Your feelings result from the messages you give yourself. In fact, your thoughts have much more to do with how you look at things in your life than what is actually happening in your life.

Once we realize that our feelings are the immediate results of our thoughts, all we have to do is control our thoughts. By doing that, we can control our emotions. I understand that it is easier said than done, however, with some awareness and a little exercise, you will be able to think good thoughts, find alternative positive answers to ambiguous stimuli and, of course, be more relaxed and peaceful.

I once had a client in her early 30s, who was complaining about her mother-in-law. It was our third session and we were practicing cognitive restructuring techniques. On this particular day, she was so furious, telling me, "I am so angry. How could she suggest that my daughter sleep over at her place? Doesn't she know that I do not tolerate my three year old to spend the night outside her own house?" I looked at her and told her: "And what gave you any idea that you had any control over your mother-in-law's mind? When during the last three sessions did I mention you having any effect on what your mother-in-law, or any other person for that matter, says or does? The only control you have is over your own mind and, thus, your own thoughts and emotions." At this, she was laughing out loud. The only thoughts we have control of are our own. That is why it is our duty to make them pleasant thoughts for our own sake, even though there will be other beneficiaries as well.

It is also worth noting that the fundamental assumption is that the individual's interpretation of an event determines how he or she feels and, accordingly, behaves. By modifying their interpretation, they can have different feelings.

For instance, you finally get the grade of an exam you have

been studying very hard for and it turns out you got a D-. If you start thinking, "I am a failure, how could I have been so stupid? I will never amount to anything," you will start feeling bad about yourself. If your internal dialogue and thoughts are, "I did my best, next time I will try harder, it happens," you start feeling relieved. Later on, you may think, "You know, the majority of the class got below average grades, so there must be something wrong with the exam. Tomorrow, I will go check it out with my friends and instructor," then the corresponding emotion will be happy. As you can see, the way you feel is directly related to the way you think.

Modifying habits of thinking that have persisted for years is no easy task. First, the person in question needs to be willing to change his or her way of thinking - I repeat, the person himself or herself, not the parent, spouse or boss. The individual has to make the conscious decision to refrain from jumping to conclusions and start picking the better alternative, choosing the more positive of possibilities time and time again until it becomes second nature to him or her.

What are you feeding your mind?

" Most folks are about as happy as they make their minds up to be "

Abraham Lincoln 1809-1865

The more we dwell on the negative, the more negative events will happen to us. I am sure you have heard plenty of stories about certain people having one misfortune after another and being caught up in a vicious cycle of bad things happening to them. I am not denying the fact that unfortunate events do occur, and sometimes in a sequence. However, I also believe that once we put our cognitions in a negative mode, we are bound to perceive more negativity around us. As the snowball picks up more and more snow on its way down the hill, you start attracting similar thoughts. The opposite is also true - when you focus on the positive, you attract positivity and see more cheerful events around you taking place.

Research shows that one of the biggest causes of depression is ruminating about something that went wrong in the past. By thinking about it, you relive it over and over again, feeding it oxygen and allowing it to go on and on.

So what are you feeding your mind: healthy positive thoughts, or a pessimistic outlook? Neither optimism nor pessimism is an accurate view of life, as neither is more realistic than the other. Both are true. But you have a decision to make. Which are you going to focus on? Which are you going to pay more attention to? Which perspective are you going to make the most dominant?

I don't think it is such a wild claim to state that an optimistic perspective promotes good health and true happiness more so than pessimism. What you look for, you will find. If you look for hatred in the world, you will find it. If you look for love in the world, you will find it. It is as simple as changing your perspective to change your experiences. It is all a matter of intention. We are not talking about some Pollyanna view, in which you deny all sadness and pain. But, you have to decide what you want to feed your mind and which perspective to emphasize.

It is all up to you!

> " Everyone thinks of changing the world, but no one thinks of changing himself "

Leo Tolstoy 1828-1910

It had been well into the fourth session of therapy when a client of mine, someone who was already aware of the techniques of cognitive restructuring, appeared at my clinic and started complaining about her husband and children (and later on, about the holidays, her in-laws, her boss and some colleagues). I told her to tell them all to come to me so I could have a talk with them and persuade them to change, then maybe she would start feeling better. As ridiculous as that sounded, it made her realize that it is easier to change our own attitude than let each and every person affect us negatively. You can't change everyone and everything around you, so you should change your view of it.

If you want to work on being positive and happy, you need to know who controls your happiness. It is a fairly common belief that a person can make another person feel bad. We often hear and make statements such as: "She made me angry", "He upset her" and "She got on my nerves". I am here to challenge this idea and propose that nobody can, in any way, ever make you feel anything. Every time I talk to people about this idea, they inevitably bring up an incident when someone upset them, saying, "They made me angry, because of what they did or said."

Cause and effect is very obvious in the physical world. You press a button and the bell rings; you turn the ignition and the engine starts running. However, cause and effect does not translate very well into the emotional world. There is no way someone can tell you something to offend you without you agreeing to it. It is just like Eleanor Roosevelt said: "Nobody can make you feel inferior without your consent." Here, I would like to remind you once again of the idea of action, thought and emotion. Outside stimuli, like people and events, can have an influence on - or trigger - our thoughts. However, it is your own thoughts, your own beliefs, your own interpretations - i.e., you and you alone - that give meaning to those influences and triggers. No one can make you feel anything. Sure, they have influence, but it is you alone that controls your beliefs. Claim your beliefs, feelings and actions as your own. Take back the reins of ownership. Remind yourself that only you are responsible for your own happiness and don't expect others to make you happy. Take responsibility for yourself.

Your attitude

> " Everything can be taken away from a man but one thing: the last of human freedoms – to choose one's attitude in any given set of circumstances, to choose one's own way "
>
> *Victor Frankl 1905-1997*

Your attitude is about beliefs or ideas you think are true about yourself, others and life. Acquired mainly as children, you could live your whole life unaware of how your attitude is affecting your thoughts, feelings and actions. Your attitude can sometimes be self-defeating, especially when thinking, "I can't change. This is the way I am", "people who are optimistic are not realistic" and "my feelings are natural reactions, not something I can control". I believe that by adjusting our attitude, we can survive insurmountable conditions. I also believe that we can thrive at what we are already doing well. No one can shape your own attitude but you. You need to work on yourself, be in touch with yourself, recognize self-defeating ideas and replace them with more encouraging ones. Your attitude is your passport in life, opening unknown doors, unlimited potential and undiscovered horizons. It is the key to living with enthusiasm. Your attitude is the precursor of the positive you.

Perhaps the story that has touched me most is one my older sister told me recently. She said she did not recall much of how life was before I was born, except that it was just Mom, Dad and her at home and that she asked our parents for a little sister. Ultrasounds did not exist at the time, and in order to save my sister disappointment, my parents tried to prepare her for the possibility of a baby boy. But, my sister refused to hear it. All she wanted was a little sister and she insisted on getting one. "And when you came," she told me, "I got my little sister, and since that day, I knew that I would get whatever I ask for - and I have!"

The Positive You!

Call it the law of attraction, call it attitude, call it positive thinking - whatever you call it, it simply works. Having a certain perspective in life will simply get you more. My sister found that out early in life - somehow she felt in her baby heart that her wishes would be granted if she wanted it badly enough. As children, we so innocently and intuitively discover truths about life that, unfortunately, we often fail to keep or follow as adults.

It is important to note that positive words contribute to creating a positive attitude. The simplest of examples is when you are asked, "How are you?" An answer such as, "Not so bad," immediately leaves a negative connotation. Now compare that to "Marvelous!" and you instantly create a positive, healthy atmosphere.

One evening, my husband and I were out having dinner with a group of friends, when we started discussing a certain topic - I don't recall the exact subject - and I gave my opinion, saying, "I hate that!" A close friend of my husband and I looked at me and said, "Anita, hate is too powerful a word. Why don't you replace it with 'dislike'?" You know, the word dislike at least has "like" in it, so it is not so negative.

We can't expect to prevent or avoid negative feelings altogether and we can't expect to experience positive feelings at all times, what is instrumental, though, is to acknowledge our feelings and to refuse to get stuck in negative ones.

The keyword is persistence.

Having a positive attitude is something you put into practice daily, when things go smoothly and when they don't, when you feel like it and when you don't. Actually, especially when you don't. You can make a habit of your positive attitude and incorporate it into your daily life.

Don't allow the craziness of everyday ups and downs get to you. Remain in touch with the good in your life, focus on the positive and choose to be optimistic. Our attitude dictates our lives.

Turn your mind into your positive world

"All that we are is a result of what we have thought"

Buddha 563-483 BC

Our minds are our worlds; our mind is our existence. It is in your mind that you choose how to live, not based on your income, physical attributions, circumstances or past.

Every single thought that occurs to me, I can either turn positive or negative. Every single judgment, analysis, prediction or wish is based on my attitude. As we all know from experience, "what will be, will be," so why not expect the good? Why not ease our minds from all the strain of negativity? What do we really have to lose? Absolutely nothing - quite the contrary, you have a lot to gain.

In my mind and with my thoughts, I have the capacity to create my own truth. I could demonize or just as well idealize any person or situation. Do you realize how powerful that is? I could dislike my mother-in-law for the usual mother-in-law stuff, or I could simply regard her as the most wonderful being because she is the one who gave life to my loving husband and brought him up. I could nag that people at work are imitating me and using my ideas, or I could feel proud to be a pioneer and role model. I could feel real sad and abandoned if my boyfriend leaves me, or I could just say he did not deserve me and it's about time I found someone who really does. I guarantee that in the simplest everyday situations, or under the most difficult circumstances, you always have the choice of picking the right attitude. In every situation you are faced with, you can always find the positive side.

You could get angry if, God forbid, you fall and break your leg and, as a result, are forced to wear a cast for four weeks. You could ask, "Anita, how can I translate this incident into something positive? How on earth can I make my mind see this as something good?" I would simply answer, "Use the time to rest and contemplate. Be alone with your thoughts.

Reevaluate your life and where you are headed, which most of us are usually too busy to think about. You may find yourself having meaningful conversations with your children because you finally slowed down and started to listen to them. Your friends may visit to wish you well and you'll realize how precious and caring all these people are. You may also catch up on a couple of movies you have been too busy to see and were dying to watch. You could do so many things that you didn't have time to take care of before and that, in the end, you may even come to like."

If I look back and reevaluate the turn of events in my own past, all I can see is that every negative situation opened the door to something great. I honestly and deeply believe that every disappointment was a turning point.

"It all depends on me" - learn to repeat and believe in this motto.

Get up each morning expecting good things to happen. Make a conscious decision to look at the good in people, the positive in situations and the best from yourself. Don't accept to be influenced by petty remarks or harassment. Rise above these things and remember your mind is yours, so keep it free of negative thoughts and influences. Remind yourself to look at things in a positive light. You can fight your melancholic moods, you can get out of your depression and you can overcome your pessimism - just make the conscious, mental decision to be positive.

CHAPTER FOUR

Live in the present

" We do not remember days, we remember moments "

Cesare Pavese 1908-1950

The Positive Yᴗu!

The beauty of our world and its people lies in their diversity.

We come across different kinds of people every day. Some constantly lament past mistakes or celebrate old glories, while others very meticulously plan their future. The past as well as the future are all part of life, however, they should not consume us so that we lose sight of everyday life or the enjoyment of simple pleasures.

You may have noticed a sizeable percentage of society living some 10, 20, or even 30 years in the past. They live their today with the memory of what it was, or what it could have been yesterday. Some live with old victories and successes while others get depressed over the unfortunate turn of events. These people all somehow lose touch with the reality of today because living in the past robs them of the present.

Those who constantly worry about the future also experience a fair share of negativity. The young university student is anxious about future possibilities and job opportunities; the pregnant woman is worried about her unborn child and her future role as a mother; the employee is concerned about keeping a job; the boss worries about being able to provide jobs. All these situations warrant our concern and worry. However, if we learn to take a step back and see the big picture, believing we are giving our best effort, then we should enjoy every second.

There are not many major events in our lives, but we are constantly preparing for them without enjoying the process, journey, or mysterious and adventurous routes that lead us there. If we calculate the hours we spend reaching our major events and the time we actually spend experiencing them, trust me, you will realize how important it is to enjoy every moment of the preparation stage because, most of the time, the anticipation is much more memorable than the event itself. As the famous American journalist and television writer Andy Rooney noted, everyone wants to live on top of the mountain, but all the happiness and growth occurs while climbing it.

The journey not the destination

> " Plenty of people miss their share of happiness, not because they never found it, but because they didn't stop to enjoy it "

William Feather 1889-1981

I'll never forget the time my husband, our then seven month old son and I decided to visit the Stonehenge ruins in England. Stonehenge is a prehistoric monument located in the English county of Wiltshire. It is one of the most famous ancient sites in the world. I was always fascinated with its majestic pictures featured in history books.

After a long drive through the English countryside - with the constant fear of being on the wrong side of the road - we finally made it to Stonehenge. We humbly went out of the car and, as I stood in front of the ruins, I was not impressed. I am ashamed to admit that I was actually disappointed. I was expecting gigantic rocks just as in the photos, yet somehow, they looked small. I was expecting a lot of surrounding green grass, but they were almost sunken in mud. I tried to rationalize the site's significance, reminding myself that the people of the time did not have the necessary tools to lift the stones, let alone carry them to the top of a hill, and that by itself was an achievement some 5000 years ago.

The moral of the story is that when I think back and recall the incident, I always remember the way to Stonehenge, how many songs we sang to our son to keep him occupied, how much we admired the beauty of the English countryside, how much of a challenge it was for my husband to manage driving on the "wrong" side of those narrow English roads, and how much we laughed when I told him, "Now I have seen enough green grass to last me a lifetime!" We managed to enjoy every moment of the journey, the process and the route, even though the final destination was not up to our expectations.

Our whole life is about the journey not the destination. Every day we live is like the route to Stonehenge and not Stonehenge itself. When we learn to look at life and live in this manner, that's when we start enjoying each and every day. We start appreciating the simple pleasures of everyday life, like kissing your children first thing when they wake up, receiving an e-mail from a friend you have not heard from in a long time, or feeling someone has genuinely complimented you - all seem more meaningful and worthwhile.

Where you are headed not where you have been

" You can never plan the future by the past "

Edmund Burke 1729-1797

Stop feeling sorry for yourself because of whatever childhood you had, whether your source of troubles was with an unfair parent, a pain in the neck sibling or at school with a hard headed teacher or bullying friends. That is all part of your past, so why waste time and energy recalling, reliving and going through all the sad scenarios in your life? The past is past; concentrate on the now and where you go from here.

Don't play the blaming game either, by thinking, "I am a failure because nobody ever listened", or "I did not continue my education because nobody really understood me at school". Ultimately, if people did actually go wrong with you in the past, it is your chance to correct that today. By constantly nagging, blaming and fault finding, you will hardly be able to direct your thoughts and energy towards becoming the better you, or the positive you. You will still be the one your guilty parties created long ago.

Try and avoid using the past tense as much as possible. Stay in the present and the near future. I want to emphasize the near future, as those who live in the distant future can be as disoriented and unhappy as those living in the past. Also, stop the internal negative dialogue.

It is here that the description of how the mind of a pessimistic, negative individual functions is pertinent. My intention is far from being mean or judgmental. I also do not wish to criticize, however, encountering so many "negative" clients has made me realize how hard it is to be "them" fulltime. I share this information to enlighten you, to warn you of the dark path of negativity that a lot of us walk on, sometimes unawares.

Hourly sessions with pessimistic clients gave me an idea of how their mind functions. You can't imagine what it is like to have that kind of frame of mind every waking hour. It is tiring, exhausting - the weather is never nice enough, the traffic never light enough, relationships never secure enough, their performance never sound enough, their country definitely not safe enough, their past not good enough and their future not hopeful enough. Can you imagine being blocked in a mind like that? There comes a time when it is not optional anymore, but rather like being caught up in an unbreakable vicious cycle. Do not allow yourself to get into that cycle. Catch yourself with your negative thoughts and replace them with more positive ones.

The only thing that stands between you and the positive you is your decision. Do not look back to the tragic, unfortunate or dull events of your past. Work on what you can achieve today. It does not matter where you come from as long as you know where you are going. Maybe that's why high school reunions were created - to give the chance to show all those nerdy bookworms what average and even below average students amounted to (which quite often is a lot!).

I am convinced that a certain amount of difficulty in the young years contributes to the formation of exceptional people. Perhaps you are familiar with someone from a novel, movie or personal friendship, who seems to come out on top with flying colors despite adversity and limited resources? How do you suppose such individuals escape the odds and achieve their life goals? Most often, it is the early experiences of adversity or loss that they remember as being instrumental in setting them on a life course. Don't be ashamed of your past, keep your head up, look ahead and never look back.

The here and now

“ Nothing is worth more than this day ”

Johann Wolfgang Von Goethe 1749-1832

One of my clients, a 50 year old self-made successful businessman, was a constant worrier, sweating the small stuff. Somewhere along the way, he discovered that the only time he stopped worrying was when he concentrated on the present moment. When he made it to my clinic, all he asked for were certain techniques to be able to live in the present moment.

As I mentioned earlier in the chapter, there are those who dwell in the past - youth, past victories or failures - while others obsess over the future, planning their lives out for the next 30 years. All this is good and fair as long as we are not totally absorbed by either the past or future, thereby losing touch of life's magical present moments.

Living the present moment is not about making a deliberate effort to stay in the here and now. It is about making a choice to ensure every minute counts in our lives and turning everyday ordinary events into extraordinary ones. It is about consciously demanding and getting the most out of your life. As the Latin adage goes, *carpe diem*, seize the day! Make your lives extraordinary. When was the last time you did something totally uncalculated, something that was completely spontaneous and just for the fun of it? Give it a try. Do something really crazy at the spur of the moment. Feel your heartbeat go faster. Feel alive.

Your life and the lives of those you love are happening now. Your life today is not a rehearsal for another life you will have later. You are here now and for a limited time. Tell the people closest to you how much you love and appreciate them. Take the time to do it today - you may not have the chance tomorrow. What a horrible life it would be to live with resentments. Treat yourself and others as if it were your last encounter with them, with love, respect and gratitude.

Living in the moment is not about concentrating on your moment to avoid painful memories or unwanted thoughts. It is about enjoying what you are doing at any given moment and making it worthwhile, concentrating on it, living it, and enjoying it fully.

Enjoy every task at hand

> " When work is pleasure, life is joy. When work is duty, life is slavery "
>
> *Maxim Gorky 1868-1936*

Enjoy what you do, do what you enjoy. I was once interrupted in the kitchen by a phone call from a friend of mine. She was perceptive enough to notice that she had caught me at a bad time from the tone of my voice. She immediately excused herself thinking I was at work. I told her, "No, I am actually home baking a cake that my children love." She sounded a bit surprised and asked, "Are you ok with that Anita? Since you are so busy at work?" I was a bit offended and my answer to her was that it was true that I enjoy my work tremendously, but I also enjoyed being a mom, cooking for my family, being there for my parents and being a socially active individual. As I was counting the number of different situations in which I was happy, I realized that I simply enjoyed everything I did and was fully taken by the task at hand.

How fair would it be to my clients during a therapy session if my mind wandered to what my kids were up to at home? How fair would it be to my children to have a mother

45

who is only physically present at the table during a nice family dinner while her mind is still at the clinic? How can I successfully play many different roles without having overlaps? Can you fully fit the role you are playing at the moment to the extent that you are completely absorbed by it? It is about giving your best in any given situation. The truth is, every action can be purposeful and fulfilling if we attach meaning to it. Take pride in what you do. Explain to yourself why you are doing what you do and why you want to do it well.

By learning to enjoy every task given to you, you are facilitating your whole approach towards your duties. Life becomes more enjoyable - "musts" and "shoulds" turn into "would like to" and "would love to". Every aspect of our being is being positive about the task at hand, so you can imagine the results that follow such an attitude.

Now, you may be asking yourself, "But, isn't this denial? Isn't this a too simplistic view of life?" The answer is, "No." You should not find it difficult to accept simple explanations to life's problems. A complicated solution does not necessarily mean it is the better option.

Do not let life slip through your fingers by living on the go. Being in one place but wishing you were in another, talking to someone as though you were answering another and keeping up a frantic pace are all unhealthy and not enjoyable. Live every moment with a firm grip on what you are doing and who you are with.

You can make a difference

> " You must be the change you wish to see in the world "
>
> *Ghandi 1869-1948*

I'll never forget the time my husband and I rushed down the subway station in Paris having just missed the train and having to wait 15 minutes for the next one. During the wait, we could not help but notice beautiful music being played from the distance. As we approached, a small crowd had gathered around a frail blind man playing some kind of strange instrument (not an unusual scene in the French subway).

We just stood there listening. You could feel the silent yet unified appreciation of the crowd, even though passersby were taking less than a minute to stop and listen before hurrying to their destination. The fellow went on and on until our attention was interrupted by an individual in the crowd who took a coin out of his pocket and placed it in the open box of the instrument. At this, every person present took a coin or two and followed the example.

Let's look back and reevaluate. While most of us probably innately appreciated and admired the talent of the musician, one person made a difference by putting his emotions into action, letting others follow and creating a change, which probably guaranteed the dinner of the subway performer. Often we go on thinking, "I am a drop in the ocean; whatever I do will not make a difference." But, I tell you that you will make a difference because you will create a change in others as they follow your lead and, thus, you will be creating change in many lives.

There are countless opportunities that allow us to make a difference every day. At times, however, we do not take action and later regret not having responded. Sometimes, we know what to do, but simply don't have the courage or inclination to go with our feelings. Do not be afraid. Just do what feels right at a particular minute. Wherever you go, leave a good impression. It could be as easy as a woman wearing a beautiful perfume so that even after she leaves a room, her scent still lingers.

Be the first to smile, be the first to extend your arm for a handshake, be the first to start a standing ovation. Pave the way for others to follow, light the path to enlighten those around you and be the change you wish to see in the world.

Move on

" The longer we dwell on our misfortunes,
the greater is their power to harm us "

Voltaire 1694-1778

If you truly want to become a positive you, it is imperative that you learn to let go of negative past experiences. We have all had our share of disappointments in life. You may have had more than your fair share of setbacks, but rather than keep on looking back and grieving over your losses, learn to move on. How do we let go of the past? Quit talking about it, quit looking back, quit reliving every negative experience. Our natural tendency is to complain. Unfortunately, lamenting over your past mistakes to other people rarely helps solve problems. Instead, it tends to drive people away. Nobody wants to hang around a person who has a self-pitying, pessimistic outlook on life.

We need to learn to let go. Disappointment is too heavy a burden to bear. If we let disappointment pile up, it leads to discouragement. Too much discouragement leads to despair - and the vicious cycle begins.

Leave the past in the past.

I am not suggesting shallow encounters to solve life's problems. What I am trying to say is that it is a pity to put your life on hold and succumb to life's difficulties, or have a fixation with some unresolved issue. We have all had our share of problems in life and we must definitely learn from them and then move on. Constantly thinking or talking about them does not give us more insight into what went wrong.

What lies ahead

> " It is not the strongest of the species that survives, nor the most intelligent, but the one most responsive to change "
>
> *Charles Darwin 1809-1882*

We are all reluctant to change. But, to resist change is to resist nature. Because time itself is moving, we need to move with it. We are often too much at ease in our comfort zone and would rather stick with the certain than jump into the unknown. However, soon enough you will realize that all people and all things around you are evolving and you need to keep pace. If you focus on what you have left behind, you will never be able to see what lies ahead.

I once had a client, let us call her Carla, who, some eight years back, had fallen in love with a fellow classmate in law school. According to her, they dated for six months, and then one day, her boyfriend came to her and revealed that he had no intention of continuing the relationship. The reason for the breakup was that he felt he was still too young for a serious commitment and needed to go out with other girls, travel and experience life more fully. Carla was devastated and decided not to let go of her boyfriend. She accepted him despite all the difficulties he put her through - including only occasionally answering her calls, dating other girls and telling her that he no longer had any feelings for her. But, she simply refused to let go of him.

Little did she notice that by refusing to move on and give new relationships a chance, she put her life on hold for eight long years. She waited for those moments of her short-lived romance to come back. Hoping against hope, she dreamt and wished and prayed until she reached my clinic. At this point, she wanted help to forget him because, as she put it, she was very much in love with him and suffering with the realization that all her past efforts to gain him back were in vain.

Our efforts at the clinic were in vain too, because one day Carla asked for an earlier appointment than our usual time. She arrived and cried her heart out. She learned that her boyfriend was going to marry a girl he had been dating for two years. At this point, Carla realized the bitter truth: everyone had moved on with their lives except her. The acknowledgement was like a slap in the face. Carla had simply refused to move on and somehow failed to adapt to her new situation. It was unfortunate that it took her so long to realize that. She failed to discover what was lying ahead and instead focused on what she had left behind.

Practice amnesia

> " Happiness is nothing more than good health and
> a bad memory "

Albert Schweitzer 1875-1965

I'll always remember my first encounter with the maternity ward at this one hospital. I was there for my regular Lamaze classes, but the midwife who taught the class had a different plan for me on that particular day. As I was approaching my due date, she thought it would be wise to introduce me to the maternity setting in order to prepare me for the big day. I was in total shock watching women screaming in pain while making all sorts of promises to themselves and their spouses that this would not only be the last time they give birth, but also the last time they would ever have a sexual encounter to guarantee the experience would never happen again!

One wonders if any of these women would agree to a second, third or fourth child if they actually recalled how much pain and suffering they endured. However, most of us automatically avoid painful memories. We have a natural tendency to discard thoughts that bring on hurtful situations. You may be asking yourself now, "But, isn't this denial?" No, it definitely is not. By refusing to relive painful memories, you help yourself overcome unpleasant experiences. It is a means of survival and the preservation of the self.

You may have noticed that when victims of a car accident, robbery, or any other traumatic event, tell their story, their heart beats faster, they sweat, they often even cry while recalling the exact details. Just by telling their story, they reenact a whole range of sad emotions. And every time they recall or retell the event, they expose themselves to the same range of emotions. So why live the tragedy over and over again? It is true that it happened once, but by not letting it go and telling your story or even thinking about it, we relive it thousands of times.

Passage of time helps alleviate even the most painful of memories. For some people, this is a bit easier than for others. We need not feel guilty letting the memory of our losses fade away with time. After all, it is a coping mechanism to survive and go on with our lives.

Make the conscious decision to let things be and move on. Don't drown in your own sorrow or misery. Keep your mind busy and active with more constructive matters. The more we keep past events alive in our minds, the more they take control of our lives. Rather than just a memory they become part of our everyday reality. Practice amnesia - trust me, it is helpful. It is not denial, it is simply a choice, the choice of rejoicing what you have today rather than what was or could have been.

The forgiving you

" I can't hate for long. It is not worth it "

William Saroyan 1908-1981

I do not recall ever being too familiar with the concept of forgiveness. I always dealt with disappointments, betrayal or any kind of misdeed by simply eliminating the person in question from my life. She or he would simply no longer exist for me. I never forgave, I simply forgot. I practiced this long enough that eventually, even if I really tried to remember certain details of what brought on this imposed exile, or termination, I could not.

I do not recall forgiveness being mentioned in any psychology book. It is through working with clients that I discovered that anger, pain, resentment and forgiveness were key issues. Some people were chronically seeking revenge and paybacks, others were victims caught up in an angry or bitter feud, and many were unable to let go of the hostility and animosity.

It is one of my dear clients who taught me the true meaning of forgiveness. Here is one amazing, yet not unusual, story of forgiveness. Sam was the younger of two boys. He always felt that both his parents favored his older brother. Since they were small children, he felt he was second best. It started off with toys - Sam always had hand-me-downs from his brother after he was tired of them. The same applied to school books. When it came to university, Sam had to attend the local one whereas his brother was sent to the best one abroad. While the older brother was given the best position in the family business, not much was left for Sam when he joined a couple of years later. At this point, Sam decided to leave the family business and start something on his own. Life went on for Sam and he thrived in his new venture. He made everybody proud of him and things were great until he got married and had two boys of his own. It is during this time that Sam felt particularly distressed. Deep inside he loved them both equally, wanted to treat them both fairly, but the memory of his own childhood was not a good reminder or a sound role model for him.

He started having all sorts of negative feelings towards his own parents, thinking about how they treated him wrongly over the years. He started recalling and reliving every unfair incident that had occurred while he was growing up. It was as if the resentment was dormant and only resurfaced when his boys were born. Sam did not want to face his parents with his feelings, he simply wanted to work it out on his own saying, "They are too old and fragile; I won't be able to forgive myself if anything happens to them." But, nevertheless, he could not go on with his daily routine of work, family and children.

We worked on a lot of issues concerning Sam's childhood. I would not be telling the truth if I said it was an easy process, but it was rewarding. It was not until Sam fully forgave his parents that he could be his normal cheerful self. He rationalized in his mind and believed that his parents wanted the best for him, that they knew all along that he was the more resilient, the more intelligent of the two brothers and that he could manage without the extra push. Sam became convinced that the attitude of his parents somehow made him stronger, and the proof of that was his ability to build and run his own empire. It was not until Sam fully understood and forgave his parents that he was able to feel comfortable and go on with his life.

So many times during the psychotherapy process, a client's ability to move forward hinges on their ability to let go of a painful past experience, which may have happened many years ago, but still manages to cause problems. If we are still hurt, we feel powerless and trapped in victimhood. Without a doubt, even if they deny it, people who choose to stay angry with someone else fall under their control. Even if blind to the fact, those who have not resolved conflicts with family members will carry that baggage into their current relationships. Forgiveness is taking positive action, reconnecting us with our own power so that we no longer feel we are victims.

Forgiveness is the greatest human capacity. By forgiving, you free yourself from what might otherwise be a never ending chain of retribution and counter-retribution.

Just like in the above example of Sam, it is about forgiving the individual for the sake of that individual, even if one cannot forgive the deed. We are all familiar with forgiving a family member or a friend because we realize they mean much more to us than the single deed we found so insulting. We cannot simply eliminate people from our lives and act as if they no longer exist or simply ignore them. When it comes to family members and genuine friendships, be open and honest. Try to understand rather than be understood and, most importantly, learn to forgive in your heart.

Forgiveness clears the past. Tell yourself that every experience you have had in life has taken you in the direction you want to go. Every experience has made you what you are today. It has turned you into a more mature, more resilient individual. Remember, no matter how sad, disappointed and angry you are today, tomorrow is another day. Holding a grudge will only harm you.

Realize that forgiveness is for your own sake and that holding on to resentment is more hurtful to you than anyone else because it keeps you from living fully in the present. Be aware that forgiveness is your responsibility. You do not really need the other person to admit that they were wrong. Waiting for that admission keeps you stuck in the past.

Last, but most importantly, learn to forgive yourself. Maybe you have gone wrong here and there. Some of us have learned the hard way that there are really no failures or mistakes, just opportunities for growth. Every experience holds a lesson for you - learn from them, don't repeat them, forgive yourself and move on.

Hope is life

> " If you could hear the whispering of the dream you would hear no other sound "

Gibran Khalil Gibran 1883-1931

First, and most obviously, hope can relieve suffering. Prisoners of war, who survive all the indignities that accompany war, tell us that those who held on to a vision of the future - be it a significant task before them or a return to their loved ones - were more likely to survive.

I am sure many of us have witnessed miraculous stories of those who were given a death sentence from doctors, but went on to survive a terminal illness because they kept their hopes high. We have heard so many cases of parents of missing children relying on hope alone to keep them going even after several decades. We are aware of the inmates who endure the silence of their lonely cells and all the difficulties of prison life with hope being their only companion.

Hope is life. Where there is no hope, seldom do we find life.

Giving up is the easiest way out of life's problems, but it only leads to a dead end. Sitting back, expecting things to take their course and passively navigating through life's ordeals seldom bring forth any solutions. Hoping, on the other hand, leads to being actively involved in life and influencing what is in store for you.

You may be thinking at this exact moment that sometimes there are things in life beyond our control and there isn't much that we can do about it. But, that is not the case. There is always something that you can do. Be courageous, be creative, be adventurous, be innovative - just be. By being actively involved, you fight and, in turn, believe in hope, and this prevents you from just passively accepting what life throws at you. You feel more in control of your life, rather than falling in the ungrateful hands of helplessness. Passivity brings on hopelessness, which is very shortly followed by helplessness. You don't want to get into that cycle. You can do a lot, you can hope against hope. It is your free will, your decision and no one can stop you from hoping. Don't ever stop believing that.

Don't expect others to think like you do

" Things and people are not what we wish them to be, nor what they seem to be. They are what they are "

Epictetus ca.55-135 BC

Expect less of others. Very often, angry feelings are generated by disappointment because of the gap between what we expect and what we get from relationships, life, or our jobs. The problem is not so much the reality of the situation, as your expectation of it. (Remember my experience with Stonehenge from Chapter Three?)

One of the greatest burdens we lay on other people is that of our expectations. We place unreal expectations on others and expect them to think like us, be like us, or meet our needs. Letting the people around us know that they are free of our expectations is a great relief for them, and by doing so, you also save yourself a lot of disappointment.

A friend of mine, a working mother of two, was once furious at her husband because, as she put it, "I have to work the same hours as he does, yet, I have to cook and take care of the children while he acts as if he is a prince in his kingdom! He doesn't help me with the chores, or anything for that matter." I told her, "Don't expect much and you will be less disappointed." A couple of months later, this friend called me up and said, "I feel much better about things now, even though I am still doing exactly what I used to do. It's just that I am not expecting much from my husband and when he actually does help me with something it makes me so happy!" The rule is simple: Life's greatest disappointments come from the highest expectations.

This does not mean, however, that you should not expect things. That is the furthest thing from the truth. We must remember that the people we live with are not mind readers or fortune tellers. Whether it is your mother, husband or children, if you don't channel your needs, how do you expect them to know what it is that you want from them? Be clear and direct; don't assume that they are supposed to know, let alone execute, what you have in mind. When we keep our demands at bay and communicate our expectations clearly, we are obviously less likely to encounter troubled waters.

Remember that your expectations are based on your background, personality, current frame of mind, principles, needs and many other factors. It is unreasonable to expect anyone to have the exact blend of traits as your own, which makes it unlikely that they will think the way you do. Of course we think differently. Each one of us is unique in the way we perceive things. What did you expect?

At university, we once had a book review project that entailed us having to find the most captivating events in the story. The next day, as each student was presenting the assignment, I noticed students differed greatly in what they thought were interesting aspects. I was pleasantly surprised to hear the same book being introduced and defined in so many different ways. What I had thought made the most sense while reading the story did not strike me as such after hearing everyone else's thoughts and analyses. It made me realize we were all right even if we thought differently.

CHAPTER SIX

Remember our time is limited

"And in the end, it's not the years in your life that count. It's the life in your years"

Abraham Lincoln 1809-1865

The Positive You!

Out of my social and clinical experience, I discovered that the happiest of all people were those who lived their lives and enjoyed each day. As Benjamin Franklin said, "One today is worth two tomorrows." Savor each moment as if it were your last, tell your parents how much you love and appreciate them. Hug and kiss your children, and no they won't get spoiled. Love, respect and appreciate your spouse, after all, this is the one person who will stay with you all the way. Our time is limited. We may have plans to do a lot, yet we waste a lot of time doing nothing. A philosopher once noted that people long for immortality but run out of things to do on a rainy afternoon.

The finality of life

> " For life and death are one, even as the river and the sea are one "

Gibran Khalil Gibran 1883-1931

According to the existential psychoanalyst, Irvin Yalom, to live life fully, one must accept that it ends. You may be questioning how the knowledge of death enriches our lives. It is the awareness of one's own finiteness that works like a wakeup call. Unfortunately for most, it comes after a confrontation with death as a result of a fatal illness, serious trauma, or simply old age. With the experience of life's transiency, we gain a different perspective whereby the real important issues gain importance and the trivial concerns in life are even more trivialized.

Nobody will live forever and when we realize that, we tend to live life more fully. It's like going on vacation to a major touristic destination. As a visitor who has limited time, you try to make the most out of your stay by visiting every possible site and attraction, places that even the locals haven't been.

The same parallel can be drawn between the limited time we have in this world and our awareness of it. The earth existed for billions of years before your arrival and will continue to do so after your departure. You are here to play your role and leave. It is your choice to decide how you wish to fill the time given to you. It is true that much was accomplished before you arrived, but much still needs to be done.

Nothing teaches us more about life than death itself. We should never forget that the people we live with are mortals. By being aware of that, we are not only enjoying every precious moment with them, we are also more prepared to lose them one day. This may sound horrific to many, but this is life and the course it takes, whether we deny it or not.

It's like a client of mine, who after losing her mother to cancer was upset that the sun was still rising at the same time in the morning. It is as though she was expecting nature to feel her sorrow and take a different course. She expected time to stand still and for nothing to happen. But, life goes on even if we expect the world to stop turning because our world has stopped turning.

We are all doing our time on this planet. The world may not be perfect, but it's the only one we've got. When you are consumed with sorrow and sadness, you think the world is not big enough to accommodate your grief. There is nowhere to run to and hide when your inner world is not at peace.

Your life is timed and every tick of the clock is time gone by. Time is precious. You don't have the luxury of a second chance, so make every minute count. Don't wait for the life threatening sickness or fatal accident to make you realize how precious life is. Redirect your life today, reprioritize your essentials and reorganize your schedule. Contemplate on letting everything you do fulfill your wishes and likes, and follow the lifestyle you want to adopt.

The Positive You!

The gift of time

> " Lost time is never found again "
>
> *Benjamin Franklin 1706-1790*

The most precious thing you can give to your loved ones is your time. Late one night, as I was doing some research on the internet, I came across a very moving story. The author is unknown, but it has touched so many people's lives while circulating the web.

A man came home from work late, tired and irritated, only to find his 10 year old son waiting for him at the door. "Daddy how much do you make an hour?" asked the boy. Greatly surprised, the father answered, "That's none of your business. Why are you asking such a thing?" "But Daddy, just tell me please! How much do you make an hour?" the boy insisted. The father, finally giving up, replied, "If you must know, I make $100 an hour." At this, the boy put his head down and asked, "Daddy, may I please borrow $50?" The father was furious and he told his son, "If the only reason you asked that is so you can borrow some money to buy a silly toy or some other nonsense, then you march yourself straight to your room and go to bed."

The little boy quietly went to his room and shut the door. The man sat down and started to get even angrier about the little boy's questions. How dare he ask such things to get some money?

After about an hour or so, the man had calmed down and started to think. Maybe there was something he really needed to buy with that $50, and he didn't ask for money very often. The man went to the little boy's room, saw his son lying in bed and told him, "I've been thinking, maybe I was too hard on you earlier. It's been a long day and I took my aggravation out on you Here's the $50 you asked for. The little boy sat straight up smiling, not knowing how to thank his father. Then reaching under his pillow, he pulled out some crumpled up bills.

The man saw that the boy already had money and started to get angry again. The little boy counted out his money and then looked up at his father. "Why do you want more money if you already have some?" asked the man. "Because I didn't have enough, but now I do. Daddy, I have $100 now. Can I buy an hour of your time? Please come home early tomorrow. I would like to have dinner with you." The father was crushed. He put his arms around his little son and begged for his forgiveness.

The anecdote illustrates how little of our time we give to the ones most precious to us. For the people we love, their time is limited too. Most of our relationships will not last forever. Think about how many Christmases you'll spend with your children before they leave home, how many more family trips you'll take, or how many more class projects you'll help your children with.

A recent personal incident shook me to the core. On one of those hectic days when I returned home from work tired, all I was thinking about was a peaceful evening with my husband and children. But, as soon as I set foot in the door, my son ran to me telling me, "You know what Christina did? She wrote on the newly painted wall in your bedroom!" I was so furious that in a split second, I was trying to find the best punishment possible for my then six year old daughter for such a devious act. I was so upset, I refused to talk to her and told her to go to her bedroom and that I would be dealing with her later. So, I carried my briefcase to my bedroom, preparing to change into something more comfortable, when I noticed a big red heart with 'Mommy I love you' written on the wall. I felt so small that I had not taken the time to know, or even understand, what had happened in my absence. I simply had pointed an accusing finger at my daughter without even trying to inquire what the problem was. I did not give the time to judge the situation myself. I went back to my daughter and hugged her. All she wanted was to show me how much she loved me after a hard day's work. I left the drawing on the wall as a reminder of the most important thing: make time for your loved ones.

The Positive YᴗU!

We are all too busy to grant time to our loved ones, but make an effort to give a minute for a smile, hug or kiss. Hold them close and let them hear you say, "You are what matters most to me in the world."

What's next?

> " I never see what has been done; I only see what remains to be done "
>
> *Marie Curie 1867-1934*

Nobody is born with a manual on how to go about life. You are the architect of your own life. You decide what is best for you. Intuitively, we all know what is good for us and we often seek advice from sources that we know will only confirm our own beliefs.

Stagnation is the enemy of creativity. Once you stop moving, you are already going backwards because everything else around you is moving. I once heard a saying that stated that you had eternity to sleep, so take full advantage of the life in you.

A famous painter was once asked, "Which one of your paintings is your favorite?" He answered, "My next one!" By constantly moving forward, you reinvent yourself, reaching heights that you never thought possible. Each time you go for something, you naturally improve it, taking it a step further and a level higher. By doing so, you reward and reinforce yourself.

I'll always remember the shopping mall that my mother used to take me to as a child. The first time I went there, I was only five years old and there was a lot of construction going on and many men working at the site. I recall holding my mom's hand very tightly, afraid I would lose her. Since then, I can't think of a time in the past thirty years when there wasn't some kind of work being done in some part of that mall - whether expanding, changing the setting or even the paint. Over the years, what used to be a tiny spot grew into a major shopping mall servicing the whole area. Up until now, it is still growing, changing and getting better. It turned out that the owner of the shopping center had a dream of creating the largest, most modern mall to leave behind for his four lovely grandchildren. He wanted them to take pride in what their grandfather had dedicated almost all his adult life to. And, every time he thought it was enough, he looked at the mall through the eyes of his grandchildren and how much they would appreciate it as adults, which prompted him to keep going on. For each and every one of us, life ought to be about growing and constantly thinking about what's next. Thinking of continuity, reinvention and rebirth motivates you to push yourself, your life and your work to higher and better places.

There is nothing worse than not having a purpose in life. I sometimes feel that in order to do everything I have in mind, I need more than one lifetime. I would love to learn new languages, travel, live in a distant civilization and learn all there is to know about the planet we occupy (and the ones that we may land on in the future). I'd also like to develop and cultivate my inner world as far as knowledge and understanding is concerned - in other words, satisfy my curiosity at all levels. It upsets me to see some people with a lot of time on their hands waste their life and just let it slip away.

It is never too late to have a dream

> "The greatest achievement was at first and for a time only a dream"

James Allen 1864-1912

We come across people in their 30s not having yet discovered what they really want to do with their lives. Others in their 40s are stuck in unfulfilling jobs, too afraid to try something new, cautious of losing their steady income to a dream or new idea, forcing them to stick to the known. Some people in their 50s look back and regret their choice of career, thinking their achievements have not been that spectacular. The question shouldn't be what have you accomplished so far, but what are you doing right now to accomplish something in the future? No matter what age group you belong to, do not determine what you are capable of based on how old you are.

We live in a time and society that is youth focused. We are led to believe that only young people have the opportunities to turn their dreams into reality. Whenever we turn to the media, we only see portrayals of either young people who are doing great things, or old people who did great things when they were young. We rarely see old people who are being recognized for achieving something late in life. We are laboring under the misconception that one must somehow be amazingly successful and wealthy before they hit 30, and every year, the age gets younger and younger.

As a result, many people tend to give up on their dreams. They believe that their time has gone and they silently settle for what they already have. But one thing that they don't realize is that creativity is ageless and dreams belong to all age groups. They can realize their dreams and fulfill their goals if they want it badly enough. We can't change the direction of the wind, but we can adjust our sails to reach our destination.

The list of late starters and late achievers is quite long and includes the likes of Charles Darwin, the famous naturalist, who discovered the theory of natural selection. He didn't have the stomach to be a physician and struggled with his clerical studies. It wasn't until he was 29 that he ended up on a boat that set him on a path to conceive his theory of natural selection. He published his first book on the subject at age 50. Voltaire was 65 when he wrote *Candide*, one of Western literature's most admired and popular works. Peg Philips, an American actress, started acting professionally in her late 60's, after retiring from a career as an accountant. She starred in the television series *Northen Exposure* which won the Golden Globe awards for best drama for two consecutive years in 1993 and 1994.

Stories about ordinary people who find their dream jobs late in life, or people who achieved success with limited resources, are also plenty. Even though many go unrecognized by the masses, they are nevertheless success stories.

A friend of mine shared this story with me. Her father dropped out of college at 20, spent some time in rehab and worked at low pay jobs until he was in his mid-30s. He then went back to college for his undergraduate degree after marriage and two children. He went on to get his Master's degree at 45 and his doctorate at 53. Today, he is a college professor.

Yes, it is possible for average people to go on to make great achievements relatively late in their life, even if they accomplished relatively little early on. More importantly, you need to ask yourself what you are going to do. Are you going to sit around for the next 40 years worrying about the things that might have been?

In the amazing song "I'm not lost, I'm exploring" Jana Stanfield and Jerry Kimbrough write: *Some people choose to live their lives on quiet avenues, while others find a place in the parade, some like me are seekers we take less traveled roads believing we can find a better way and though I get discouraged, I won't be turning back, I have joy as my compass and faith as my map.*

Passion is the key to greatness. Find out what you are passionate about, pursue that relentlessly and create the life you wish for.

The way most people take failure is by misjudging their abilities, belittling their worth and value, not believing or not even having dreams. Merely having a dream means you have the desire to fulfill it. Our dreams need not stay dreams. Think big, dream big. It does not take any more energy to expect to be the best housewife, the finest cook or the most capable artist. Just dream of it, hope for it and be enthusiastic about it.

The Positive You!

The wise you

> " Wrinkles should merely indicate where smiles have been "

Mark Twain 1835-1910

I will never forget the conversation between my son and my daughter as I was driving them to a friend's house one day. My son was telling me: "Mom, do you feel that time passes fast when we go to school?" I told him yes. My son, soon to enter his teenage years and already showing signs of a much-desired independence, continued, "Mom, I wish time would go by fast so that I can become an adult and drive and have my own home." At this point, my seven year old daughter interrupted, saying, "I don't want the time to pass quickly because I don't want to get old!"

The reality of getting old is displeasing to almost everyone. In today's society, everyone wants to look young and attractive. We want to stay independent and in touch with modern times. We fear physical decline and dread dependency and all the indignities of old age that we think inevitably accompany getting older. Because of this, we often look at aging as a negative process.

Time is a precious thing. The years teach you so much that the days never knew. Use your time wisely and live a life of no regrets. The only way you can achieve that is to live your life fully.

There is nothing more distasteful than reaching your golden years having regrets, aware of all the lost opportunities, including the vacations you never took, the wild and exotic places you never traveled to and the fun you missed by spending more time at the office than was needed. Twenty years from now, you will be more disappointed by the things that you didn't do than by the ones you did. So, sail away from safe harbors, widen your horizons, risk untested waters, explore, dream and discover!

The wise you is also about knowing that no matter how you have lived your life, there are always a couple of things that you would have probably liked to do differently. So what? We all know from experience that when looking back on things we have done, we are bound to find a lot not to our liking. Even Pablo Picasso, in his later years, was not allowed to roam an art gallery unattended because he had previously been discovered trying to improve on one of his old masterpieces. Remember that times change, so be fair to yourself. Put yourself back in exactly the same context you were in then so that you don't judge your past by what you know today. If given the chance, you may still end up doing exactly what you did then.

The saddest among the elderly are those who feel that life just passed them by. The more resentments you have, the stronger your bitterness; the more regrets, the harder your present situation. There is no escape - we are all going down the same road and none of us is getting younger. But, I am preparing for my old age today, not just in financial terms, but also with regards to health issues, family matters, my emotional well-being and ensuring I live my life right and to the fullest.

Constantly worrying about getting old is another common problem faced by a lot of middle-aged men and women. It is a problem that brings to mind a friend of mine in her late 30s. As far back as some fifteen years ago, this woman has been worried about getting old. Happily married with two children, she constantly refused to listen to reason when discussing this topic. One time, my patience was running thin and I told her bluntly, "You know, you will finally get there anyway, but you are wasting your youth worrying about aging. Enjoy today, because even if you are worried, anxious, or peaceful about it, it will still come. Or sadder still, you may not even make it. Did you ever consider that? So, make the best out of your life."

I admit it was harsh, but it did the trick. She did contemplate on the possibility of not even making it to old age, and only then did she realize that it was indeed a blessing to grow old. Thinking about how lonely her husband would be and how sad it would be for her grandchildren not to have her around was a wakeup call.

The idea of "old" is always fifteen years older than your current age. To a five year old, someone 20 is practically ancient, whereas 35 seems middle-aged to a 20 year old, and if you are 30, 50 is beyond imagination.

A few years ago, I was paying a visit to my maternal grandmother, who at the time was in her 70s and still had her own 90 year old mother living with her. When my grandmother started describing how difficult life had become for my great-grandmother, I noticed that my grandmother did not consider herself old at all! I had wrongly assumed that most people in their 70s consider themselves old, obviously I was wrong. I also realized that not all the elderly are the same - some even belong to different generations.

Every age has its own challenges and joys. It is the different experiences of life that come with each passing year. Most people don't think of themselves as the age they are.

CHAPTER SEVEN

Honor yourself and all beings

" Reputation is what other people know about you. Honor is what you know about yourself "

Lois McMaster Bujold 1949-

The Positive You!

I have always had the ultimate respect for all living things. Respect for others is based on self-respect. It is value that makes the world a more decent, peaceful and civilized place. Start the process today. It is not wrong to treat yourself with high levels of respect; quite the contrary, you would be honoring yourself and setting a good example for others to follow. Just as anger breeds more anger and aggression more aggression, respect begets more respect. Once again, it all starts with you.

Create an atmosphere of honor and respect wherever you go. Be thoughtful with your words, helpful with your remarks, generous with your time and cautious with your judgments. As the saying goes, two thirds of what you see is often behind your eyes. Making a bad judgment about a particular individual does not necessarily make that person bad. Give people the benefit of the doubt; let them remain innocent until - hopefully not - proven guilty. Don't judge their good, or not so good, nature based on some rumor or piece of gossip. Don't be a harsh critic and reach the point of no return. Save face.

The fragile you

" The greatest weakness of all is the great fear of appearing weak "

Jacques Benigne Bossuel 1627-1704

The time we will fully be able to understand and manage our lives is when we recognize how fragile we are. Certain unpleasant situations are unavoidable and, yes, none of the previously mentioned steps will help you see the bright side, think positively or be able to help alleviate the pain. With the realization of our emotional weaknesses, we are in touch with our human side, the vulnerable being, the inner most self that is often shaky, only surfacing in the face of adversity. It is this self that we are most afraid to reveal, that we almost try to disguise, and which could, despite your efforts, reveal to the world how fragile you are. However, once you realize that you are not the only one, and that all the people you have encountered, or ever will, are exactly the same, you will feel more at ease. Have you ever wondered why we always avoid crying in public? Think of all the other feelings and behaviors we openly portray - like anger, embarrassment, disgust, intolerance and impatience - and then think why being sad and crying are almost always reserved for when we are alone.

Our biggest battle is eliminating negative self-appraisals. I don't mean rational self-evaluations, but the habits of negative thinking that are so ingrained that most of us are not even aware of them. Who says it is not okay to feel weak or vulnerable? There is no need to wear a mask of gaiety at all times. I have the right to be sad from time to time and that does not make me socially weak or unacceptable. I am entitled to feel fed up. So what?

Learn to acknowledge your true feelings that pertain to whatever situation you happen to be in. Do not be ashamed. Just as you have the right to persist in your happiness, you have the right to off days too. Don't make excuses for yourself or anybody else!

We are only human

" Remember that every man is a variation of yourself "

William Saroyan 1908-1981

Take just any man and ask, "Who is he?" It is difficult to answer such a question, because to the doctor he is a patient, to the politician a vote, to the mailman an address, to the biologist a specimen and to the shop owner a customer. Apart from our immediate circles, we all look at each other from the outside. It is absolutely normal that we don't attach feelings to strangers. We treat them just as people, but we also often have low tolerance for them, especially while driving. We sometimes even dislike them without even knowing them. But, this should not be the case.

I believe that all humans are born with a good nature. Somewhere along the way, we learn that showing and being in touch with that good side is only hurting us because people around us might be taking advantage. We think that it is not right to be too transparent and in order to "protect" ourselves, we deeply bury this good nature - so deep that sometimes we even forget it exists. The façade we like to portray is the strong me, the confident me, the invincible me. But, it's not wrong to acknowledge humanity with all its weaknesses and vulnerabilities. It's not a crime to feel and mourn losses. All emotions need to be lived through and then we need to let go of them. Just like we live enjoyable moments, we also need to live those of fear, anxiety and loss, and then move on.

Life cannot be a long train of positive events and feelings, no matter how much we want that. We are only human and in the face of adversity, we will sometimes be helpless, hopeless, depressed and even suicidal. But such feelings should be followed by an action plan. Take control again by using positive strategies. Every negative event should be a turning point in our lives, when we grab the opportunity, seize the chances and make positive changes. Once again, take advantage of even the ugliest of events and turn it around.

With the realization that every person has weaknesses and we are all trying to make it in this world no matter what the outer mask is portraying, we tend to empathize more with the difficulties of others. We become more understanding and compassionate. We seek to understand then be understood.

Look up to people whenever you can, but never down.

Erroneously attributing blame is one of the most common, yet most unfair, mistakes that we make in our social encounters. When things go wrong with us, we most often attribute it to things outside ourselves. For example, if you are late for an important appointment or date, you may blame the traffic, bad weather, a policeman, or any other number of things except for, of course, yourself. Suppose it was your husband, boyfriend or colleague who was late. You would immediately start thinking, "that's how much he cares", "he is never on time", or "he is not punctual". In short, when things go wrong with others, we attribute it to that person.

Don't be too hard on others. Give people the chance to explain and listen to what they have to say. Concentrate on their words, rather than only partially lending a listening ear while preparing what to say next. See the good in people and choose to concentrate on the good. The kind of treatment you usually receive from a person is very much related to the way you approach that individual. It's hard to imagine that someone would address you negatively if you were kind and gentle in your approach. A nice word, a genuine compliment and deserved praise are priceless. So, be generous with your positive approach towards others and soon it will all come back to you.

Be your best friend

" To be alone is the only real revolution. To accept that you are alone is the greatest transformation that can happen to you "

Osho 1931-1990

We seek approval and many times, we define ourselves by how others view us. We even take on different characteristics with different people. As a child, I always played the guessing game when my mother received a call. From her tone of voice, her choice of words and expressions, I almost always ended up guessing who was on the other end of the line. My mom unconsciously picked up the attitude of the person she was talking to. We sometimes do this in subtle ways, but at other times we risk losing our individuality, especially in relationships in which we find ourselves conforming more and readjusting our principles. We may eventually feel let down and hurt, realizing that our expectations were set too high.

It is all about you, you and you! I can't stress this enough. You need to feel you are in control. You have to believe in yourself. You must boost yourself. In other words, start treating yourself the way you think your best friend, ideal spouse or perfect lover should treat you.

Inner strength comes from trusting yourself, having faith in your abilities and knowing that you can conquer anything if you really put your mind to it.

Being your best friend also means keeping your innermost feelings, personal experiences and especially your secrets to yourself. This may sound hard to some and shocking to others, but it is crucial. A very close friend of mine taught me that if you cannot keep your own secret, you cannot expect a friend to keep it for you. It is actually ironic that my friend gave me advice on the benefits of keeping things from friends.

Except for some cases, most people are best able to solve their problems by themselves. This is because nobody can really understand your problem, the feelings attached to it as well as your personal experiences and background quite the same way as you do. Therefore, the advice, or solution, given may not be the best one for you. Deep down, you have the answers, but need to find the courage to execute them or to make the right decision. As they say, the right decision is always the more difficult one.

I always tell my clients about the "solid self", one that does not sway left and right with the first signs of wind. One that is receptive to comments and criticism enough to learn from them and turn them to his or her advantage. One that is solid enough not to be affected with a word or remark. One that is in control despite controversies.

One that is not on the defensive or the offensive. This is what we ought to reach to be strong yet sensitive as well as honest yet assertive, happy yet aware and concerned yet hopeful. It is very powerful to rely on oneself. A good support system is important, but more important is to know how to survive alone.

I had a 23 year old client who dreaded being alone, even for a minute, in her waking hours. But, that was not the reason she headed to my clinic. Her presenting problem was her dissatisfaction with her job as a translator in a foreign company. Throughout the sessions, I discovered that this young woman was avoiding being alone. She made sure she had a full agenda on any given day, even though the whole process was exhausting. But, the alternative of being left alone with her thoughts was distasteful to her. We went through a lot of discussions and, as it turned out, she simply did not want to think her own thoughts or feel her own feelings. She needed outside stimuli to keep her mind busy. She needed a flight of people bombarding her with their own stories to keep her mind off her own sad story. After a great deal of resistance, she finally decided to share her story with me.

Two years back, she had a car accident that involved a 12 year old boy. The boy's injury to the legs was so serious that he ended up in a wheelchair. The most painful part of it was that he was her brother and the guilt had not left her alone since that day. She was not strong enough to face and accept the tragedy, but by refusing to deal with her emotions, she got herself into a never ending cycle of guilt and avoidance.

Even in the worst of situations, we need to be in touch with ourselves. You can run away from the whole world, but you cannot run away from yourself. Be at peace with yourself, mind and body. Be in touch with your innermost feelings. Do not be afraid to face your fears. You are capable. As I mentioned in Chapter One, your relationship with yourself is the central and most important relationship in your life. Remember that and work on it every day. We all have to learn to be our own best friend because we can easily turn into our own worst enemy - and no one can take you out of that shell but you yourself.

People and you

> "Be the inferior of no man, nor of any man be the superior"
>
> *William Saroyan 1908-1981*

Even though values and norms are highly cultural, there are universal values that make up the underlying silent structure of all societies. One such universal value is friendship. Humans are social beings - social interaction and complexities are an integral part of our daily lives.

The way you treat life and the people in your life is basically a habit. No matter what your current code of conduct is, you can always retrain your thinking and, thus, your behavior vis-à-vis other people. That in of itself does not keep us free from misunderstandings. There is so much room for misinterpretation in our social life, but if we choose to see the good in people, then we would try to understand rather than be understood. As a result, we give individuals the benefit of the doubt and save ourselves a lot of trouble.

If I had to pick one life lesson of the many my mother taught me while growing up, I would choose her instruction to be good in life and be good to people because good always wins, no matter what. The passage of time is the dormant proof of the reality of this statement.

See the good in people. Widen the range of tolerance, patience and understanding. There are many more good people on this earth than bad. Look beyond little thought-less or careless acts and do not take them personally. Be the bigger person and try not to dwell on them. Remember, it is destructive to your own peace of mind to carry negative thoughts.

Choose right over wrong and good over bad - you always have a choice. Deep inside we know which way to go. Choose to speak in favor of someone rather than gossip, because your importance is not increased by belittling another. Compliment a person for a job well done. Everyone you meet has something to teach you, so be humble and open, and give people the chance to enlighten you. You'll be amazed at the most unexpected lessons life teaches you in the most unlikely places.

While we all know that a friend in need is a friend indeed, I would like to share with you the flip side of the coin. Be there for your friends, not just in their sad moments, but even more so during their happy times. I am sure a lot of people will disagree with me, however, I believe genuine friends and their devotion to us show more when we are celebrating success and are in a happy moment, rather than in times of misery. Just like Oscar Wilde said, "Anyone can sympathize with the sufferings of a friend, but it requires a very fine nature to sympathize with a friend's success."

Choose the people in your life with caution and care. We are born to families, but we give birth to friendships. Carefully choose the people you call your friends, because a lot of your happiness is shared with them. They will have a lot of influence over you in terms of attitude, outlook and life in general.

At one time or another, you may come across people who are angry and negative all the time. If you happen to live or work with someone like this, be cautious because they can crush your spirit to the point where you begin to feel hopeless and defeated, and no matter what you do, you feel it is not good enough. Do not let such people make you think that you are the cause of their problems or unhappiness. Negative people need to take ownership of their own issues.

I am not against friendships, but I am for friendships with boundaries. Personal space is a valuable commodity - your independence should not be at stake. Remember the "solid self" mentioned earlier in the chapter.

It is undeniable that disclosure may relieve you from some of the stress of bearing a problem, but it is also worth noting that it is risky. No matter how tempting it is for you, and no matter how trustworthy the person in front of you may seem, be careful of how much you reveal and how soon. The opposite is also true. Do not casually allow people to confide in you. Keeping a person's secret is a big responsibility. Sometimes, at the spur of the moment, someone may want to open his or her heart to you, often regretting it the following day. Confiding is powerful for both parties. We are all too willing to listen, give advice or even offer help, but we should remember that sharing a secret turns you into part of that secret and listening to a problem also makes you part of the problem. You run the risk of becoming part of the past and, very possibly, it ends up being an uncomfortable or dreaded past. It could create an awkward atmosphere for both involved parties. So, be wary of how much, how soon and how far you or the other party shares information. Once again, you should set the limits.

Being sociable, kind and friendly does not entail sharing your intimate details or personal issues. The best of friends must still keep respectful boundaries and points of return. Anyone trying to push for more information or details goes from being caring to being curious, and an uninvited curiosity is seldom a good recipe for friendship.

No doubt, we all have a side to us that we don't want to share, even with people we have been living with for 30 or more years. A friend once told me about a certain fellow who had been happily married to his high school sweetheart for about 40 years. He felt the most content when alone in his car singing out loud to one of his favorite songs. As he put it, the feeling was not the same in the presence of his wife. They had shared so much in their years together, but there was a small part of him that still needed to be alone. The moral of the story is that even though the people closest to us are close, they are not us. We need our space, privacy and individuality.

Don't let anyone be intrusive or intimidating - it is your right to set boundaries with others, including your significant other, friends and even your parents and children.

There is a happy middle ground between unrestricted boundaries and too much closeness in all social situations. Be the positive force in life and learn to separate yourself from your surroundings by setting healthy, vital boundaries. You are entitled to have your personal space just as you are entitled to have meaningful relationships. One does not cancel out the other. It's quite the opposite: one complements the other, so don't let anyone convince you otherwise.

Be the positive example of all social affairs.

Don't let your possessions possess you

> "The greatest possession is self-possession"
>
> *Ethel Watts Mumford 1878-1940*

You are not your possessions, nor are you the sum of your possessions. You are only you. You would be amazed by how little one can live with. We become so accustomed to our material things that we become addicted to them, as though life cannot go on without them. But, it has been shown time and time again that possessions do not make us happier or more fulfilled. After the initial, basic needs are met, money and material stuff do not add much to our happiness. We do not become better or worse by what we own. That does not dictate our worth.

I had a client, who, every time he felt lonely or bored, went out to buy something for himself or his house. He described it as though he was filling a void. After several therapy sessions, he revealed that as a child, his parents worked abroad and he spent several years in a boarding school, only seeing them during summer vacations. Apart from those visits, the only kind of attention he was given was in the form of gifts he regularly received during Christmases, birthdays or special occasions. The boy was always rewarded with material items. Parental attention and affection came in gift wrapped packages for this boy until he learned to associate his self-worth with possessions.

Another side to unhealthy possessions is addictions. I never really believed in any kind of addiction, whether food, cigarettes, chocolate, drugs, or compulsive buying, among others. How can anyone allow a material thing take control of him or her? I somehow could not accept becoming dependent on a material thing that would even partially control my life. To free one's self from dependencies is to be whole. It is taking back full charge of your life and being on top of things. It is a big challenge to face addictions, but when you succeed, you feel in full control of your life, as if the worst case scenario took place and you were able to defeat it. You feel that no matter what else comes your way, you now know you can overcome it.

You are a worthy individual because you are you, not because of what you possess. Your personality, individuality and spirit make you who you are, not your house, car or designer clothes. Your happiness is a result of your attitude rather than external factors.

I don't understand why people put so much effort on what is on the outside without nurturing their inside and self-awareness as well as their mental and emotional well-being. Just like we take a few minutes a day checking our appearance in the mirror, we should also take a few minutes to check who and how we are on the inside. We should be in touch with our inner self and learn to listen to the little voice inside of us. We should validate our feelings and trust our instincts. Fight negativity, be whole, be self-reliant, just be who you are without the masks and the pretenses.

Remember, other people are similar to us, it does not matter what their sex, race or age. Look beyond a person's outward appearance, profession or status and see the real inner beauty he or she possesses.

Look for solutions!

> " In the middle of difficulty lies opportunity "

Albert Einstein 1879-1955

Life is difficult. It is necessary to accept that life in general is full of difficulties and adversities. This recognition is the first step. Problems, difficulties or challenges should not intimidate us. In fact, confronting and solving problems - no matter how painful the process - makes us grow.

Learn to separate yourself from your problems and don't become consumed by them in such a way that you cannot concentrate on anything else. I have often heard from clients that as a result of focusing on an argument with a significant other, parent, friend or co-worker, they could no longer concentrate on even the most trivial of tasks. In such cases, all you can think about is the fight or argument, replaying it over and over in your mind. Learn to treat problems as part of the realities of life.

Problems will come and go, but during the process, we should not lose ourselves in the problem. We so easily become the victims of our own minds, giving our full energy to one problem, that in the end, we lose track of things. Unfortunately, a lot of the time, we also lose track of ourselves.

Life throws all sorts of obstacles in our way. The way we handle these difficult situations tells us a lot about our personalities and how we cope with problems. This idea is well illustrated in the following story. There was once a workshop training social workers. The speaker presented the participants with a paragraph and asked those who were right handed to copy the whole paragraph with their left hand and all those who were left handed to copy it with their right hand. As this small experiment went on, each person reacted in a different way. Some gave up right from the beginning, some were angry with the difficulty of the task, some were quietly trying to concentrate and give it their best shot, and some were trying to cheat. The purpose of the experiment was to make each one realize how they were handling an unexpected difficult situation. Finally, those who put their mind to it succeeded despite the difficulty. Nagging and feeling sorry for oneself did not get anyone any results. And, of course, cheaters were detected and they felt humiliated.

Difficulties and friction are the accompaniments of life. If everything was smooth all the time, we would have nothing to do.

When faced with problems, we often feel lonely, thinking we are the only one having such difficulties. Or, we tend to exaggerate and make it into an unbearable catastrophe. However, if we look around us, we find people in much worse conditions. As St. Augustine said, "I cried for boots, till I saw a man who had no legs."

Every problem we encounter leads us to one of two choices. Either we choose to be victorious, or we choose to be a victim. Either we choose to be responsible for the life we create, or we shrink from our responsibility by blaming others for our failures and unhappiness.

Look for solutions. Look for the answers. You can turn every bad situation to your advantage. A friend of mine was relocated by his company to an office that was an hour's drive from his home. At first, he was upset at the idea of losing two hours of his day on the roads, but he later found a very helpful solution to his problem. He had always dreamt of learning Italian and never quite found the time to fit it in his busy schedule. So, he bought a CD kit to learn the language in the quiet privacy of his car, away from the office and home while driving back and forth from work. Soon, he came to look forward to his driving time because besides realizing his dream of learning Italian, he was also enjoying those two extra hours.

You can be creative and proactive in your approach to finding solutions to your problems, and by doing so, you will find life more interesting as well as more exciting.

Don't ever give up

> " Never, never, never give up "

Winston Churchill 1874-1965

Stories of courage, tales of heroism, human beings fighting against their dark destiny and still going on, are all pretty common themes in books and movies. They are reenactments of our innate tendency to fight in order to preserve ourselves against environmental threats or human indignities and, sometimes, even our own wrong decisions and choices. As children, when we were told or read such stories, deep inside we all identified with the hero and secretly pretended to be him or her - we were the princess, we believed we could fight and would be fought for, and eventually, would be the winner. All children, without exception, believe that, but unfortunately, as adults, we sometimes lose, or are forced to lose, this belief as we encounter the real world with its real issues.

As we pass by a subway station in any part of the world, we see the homeless looking for shelter. The only reason why these people ended up there is because somewhere along the way, they did not have the courage to fight. They proved too weak in the face of unfortunate events and surrendered to the bitter reality of almost nonexistence. They are human beings just like the rest of us, but we look at them with disdain and sometimes even pretend that they don't exist. Even if we do acknowledge their existence, we don't think that they have feelings and treat them as if they were different from us; we tell our children not to stare at them. The only difference between us and the homeless is that they simply gave up on themselves. Yes, your life and the quality of your life depends on every decision that you make, every fight you were too afraid to battle and every loss you accepted without trying and trying again for success. This is what your life is about, to be ready to go all the way, not to succumb to life's difficulties and not to readily accept defeat.

The Positive You!

While every one of us will have problems and challenges, for some, life can sometimes become extremely tough. To overcome obstacles, we need to dig deep and find the strength, determination, persistence, resilience, courage and positive mental attitude to persevere.

Don't ever give up on life and don't ever give up on yourself. No matter how hard your problems seem, no matter how sad you feel, there is a ray of hope for everyone. Bring out the positive in you to fight those fears and moments of anger, silent despair, self-doubt or uneasiness to overcome times of crisis and hopelessness. Do not lose touch of who you are and where you are going. Remember, you own your mind and thoughts, so make them positive and be optimistic - worrying never solved anything. Rise above things.

We are each capable of creating our own reality and shaping our own destiny. People who complain that they were born into the wrong family, country, race or situation are merely admitting defeat, or not accepting that they are individually responsible for their position in life.

Stay passionate about life. Whatever it is that you are doing, if you do it with more passion, you will do it better. Turn the vicious cycles into vital cycles, ones that will only bring more of the positive in life and in you.

Life is worth the fight despite all the severe trials we will face.

Don't ever, ever give up on yourself. You have this one life to live, no second chances, so make the most and best out of it. Even when in doubt, life will turn around and embrace you if you just give yourself that chance. No matter how difficult your current situation is, and how hopeless it looks to you today, tomorrow is another day with new hopes, new beginnings, new ideas and new horizons. Let the positive in you come forward, reminding you what a miraculous, unique and special individual you are.